Ancient Egypt

Don Nardo

KidHaven Press

KidHaven Press, an imprint of Gale Group, Inc.
P.O. Box 289009, San Diego, CA 92198-9009

Library of Congress Cataloging-in-Publication Data

Nardo, Don, 1947–
  Ancient Egyypt / by Don Nardo.
    p. cm. — (History of the world)
Includes bibliographical references and index.
Summary: Discusses the history of ancient Egypt including the
relationship between pharaohs and gods, worship and burial
customs, the rise and fall of the empire, and the later discovery
of the pharaoh's tombs and their contents.
  ISBN 0-7377-0774-7 (hardback : alk. paper)
  1. Egypt—Civilization—To 332 B.C.—Juvenile literature.
[1. Egypt—Civlization—To 332 B.C.] I. Title.
  DT61 .N327 2002
  932—dc21

2001002211

Contents

Chapter One
The Lives of Egypt's God-Kings   4

Chapter Two
Egyptian Worship and Burial   14

Chapter Three
The Rise and Fall of the Egyptian Empire   22

Chapter Four
The Modern Rediscovery of Ancient Egypt   30

Notes   38

Glossary   40

For Further Exploration   42

Index   44

Picture Credits   47

About the Author   48

The Lives of Egypt's God-Kings

One of the world's earliest and greatest civilizations grew up in Egypt, the land occupying the northeastern corner of Africa. Egypt became famous partly for its massive stone monuments. These included huge, splendid palaces in which the Egyptian kings, called **pharaohs**, lived, and also giant statues of these rulers. But most famous of all are the pyramids. The pharaohs erected the pyramids as tombs for themselves and sometimes for their wives and children. The largest of these structures still stand at Giza, near Egypt's modern capital, Cairo. The ancient authors listed them among the "seven wonders of the world," and people today continue to view them with awe.

Ancient Egypt was also renowned for the mighty Nile, the world's longest river. It rises in the highlands of east-central Africa and flows some 4,130 miles to Egypt's northern coast, where it empties into the Mediterranean Sea. As it still does today, in ancient times the Nile dominated the country. Very dry, mostly lifeless deserts make up more than 90 percent of Egypt's territory. So the moist, green strip of land running along the Nile's banks, making up the other 10 percent, stands out starkly. This land is very fertile and supports large-scale agriculture.

It is not surprising, therefore, that the vast majority of ancient Egyptians lived near the Nile's shores. They became dependent on the river, in fact. Each year it gently flooded its banks, irrigating their crops. It also provided them with the water they needed to drink, cook, bathe, and wash their clothes. In addition, the river was a sort of liquid highway on which

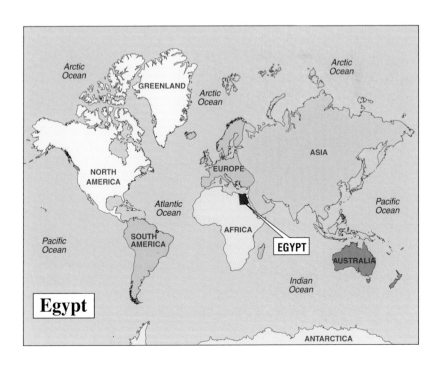

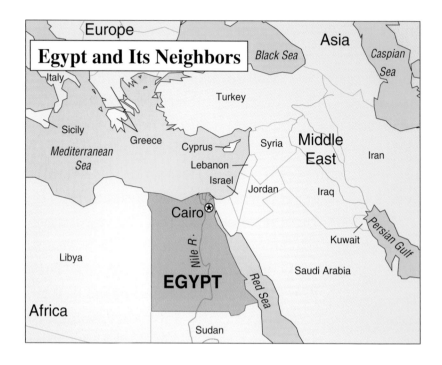

they sailed or rowed small boats from town to town. To the Egyptians the Nile was more than just a river; it was a life-giving entity. And they came to respect and revere it so much that each year they sang the "Hymn to the Nile." "Hail to you, O Nile," it began,

> that issues from the earth and comes to keep Egypt alive! . . . When the Nile floods, offerings [**sacrifices** to give thanks] are made to you, oxen are sacrificed to you, great obligations are made to you. . . . And offerings are made to every other god, as is done for the Nile, with prime incense, oxen, cattle, [and] birds. . . . So it is "Green are you!". . . So it is "O Nile, green are you, who makes men and cattle to live!"[1]

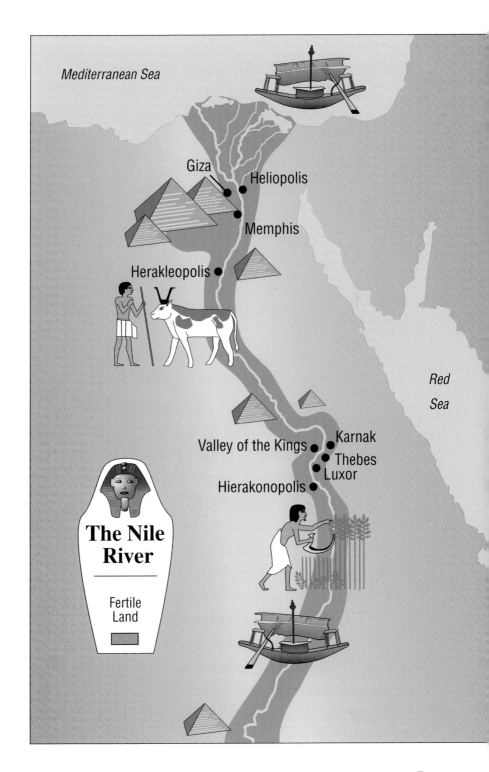

Mediterranean Sea

Giza

Heliopolis

Memphis

Herakleopolis

Red

Sea

Valley of the Kings

Karnak

Thebes

Luxor

Hierakonopolis

The Nile River

Fertile Land

The World's First Nation

Another distinction ancient Egypt could claim was that the world's first true nation rose within its borders. This crucial event took place sometime between 3150 and 3100 B.C., roughly fifty-one centuries ago. Before this, two separate, smaller kingdoms had existed in Egypt, one in the south, the other in the north. Menes, a powerful king of the southern realm, unified the two kingdoms into a single nation, in the process making himself the first pharaoh. To emphasize to his people the importance of unity, Menes erected a new capital city—Memphis. It stood at the boundary between the former rival kingdoms. He also adopted a crown that combined the main features and colors of the crowns worn by the leaders of the two original kingdoms.

Egyptian Royalty

The first of many Egyptian dynasties was established by Menes. Each **dynasty** was composed of a series of rulers belonging to one family line and over the following three thousand years, more than thirty royal dynasties ruled Egypt, producing a total of over two-hundred pharaohs. Like rulers in all times and places, each had individual abilities, strengths and weaknesses, and aims for himself and his nation.

But almost all the pharaohs held one important attribute in common. Their people viewed them as living gods. Each pharaoh was believed to be a child of Ra, the god of the sun, and therefore both different and better than other mortals. So the pharaoh's word was law. When he gave an order, everyone had to obey him. Moreover, tradition held that he was wiser, braver, and physically stronger than any of his subjects. This was rarely, if ever, true, of course. But that was the pharaoh's official image, and many Egyptians over the ages believed it.

A Privileged Life

The everyday lives and surroundings of these Egyptian "god-kings" naturally reflected their power. While most of their subjects were poor and lived in huts and shacks, the pharaohs enjoyed the advantages of great privilege and wealth. As royal princes, future Egyptian kings grew up in magnificent palaces filled with works of art and all manner of luxuries. They

A wall painting shows foreigners bearing gifts for an Egyptian pharaoh.

had numerous servants who took care of all their needs. Some servants even bathed and dressed them. And each prince received the finest education available. This included learning how to read and write, the proper use of the sword and other weapons, and how to receive visitors at the royal court.

A pharaoh-to-be also accompanied his father, the reigning pharaoh, on hunting trips. Letters carved in stone have survived telling about such royal hunts. In one message, the pharaoh Thutmose III, who reigned for fifty-four years beginning in 1479 B.C., claimed he bagged 120 elephants. "No king has ever done such a thing since the world began,"[2] he boast-

This modern drawing shows what the inside of an Egyptian palace looked like.

ed. Another inscription, by one of Thutmose's attendants, recalls a dangerous moment on the hunt: "The
biggest elephant . . . began to fight before the face of
His Majesty. I was the one who cut off its trunk while
it was still alive, in the presence of His Majesty." [3]

When the pharaoh died, his son took his place.
Priests dressed as various gods led him to the throne
room. There, amid much ceremony, the country's
leading citizens watched him receive the double
crown of Upper and Lower Egypt and become the
new god-king. After that, he moved into his father's
comfortable rooms. One of these rooms led to the
Balcony of Appearances, which faced into a huge outside courtyard. On his coronation day, and on later
festive occasions, the new king stood on this platform
to let his people see and worship him.

The Power to Mobilize a Country

Perhaps the most famous examples of the praise,
power, and privilege enjoyed by the Egyptian
pharaohs were their grand tombs—the pyramids.
These rulers erected more than ninety pyramids in
all. Most, including the giant ones at Giza, were
created during the Old Kingdom. This is the name
modern scholars call the five-century-long period
lasting from about 2700 to 2180 B.C.

The largest pyramid of all was that built by the
pharaoh Khufu. He reigned from 2589 to 2566 B.C.
The structure, often called the "Great Pyramid," mea-
sures about 756 feet at the base of each of its four sides

One of Egypt's famous pyramid tombs rises at Giza, near the modern capital of Cairo.

and covers an area of more than 13 acres. Its original height was 481 feet, almost half as tall as New York's Empire State Building. The Greek historian Herodotus visited Egypt in the fifth century B.C., about two thousand years later, and interviewed some Egyptian priests. They told him that Khufu's pyramid "took twenty years" to build. "It is of polished stone blocks," Herodotus wrote, "beautifully fitted, none of the blocks being less than thirty feet long."[4] The structure required about 2.3 million of these blocks in all, each weighing an average of two and a half tons.

Quarrying these stones, dragging them to the work site, and lifting them into place was an enormously difficult task. Lacking the advantages of modern machines, the Egyptians relied on abundant manpower, patience, and ingenuity. Teams of workmen placed the stone blocks on rows of logs, which acted as rollers. To get the blocks up to the pyramid's higher levels, the workers piled up huge earthen ramps around the structure. When the work was finished, they removed the earth, revealing the finished pyramid.

The notion that these workers were slaves is a common misconception. Instead, they were free men who willingly did the work out of duty and love to their country and god-king. The power and image of Egypt's early pharaohs was so great that they could mobilize an entire country to help a single person reach the afterlife.

Chapter Two

Egyptian Worship and Burial

From the loftiest pharaoh to the poorest peasant, all ancient Egyptians were religious. And they worshiped a large number of gods. The people erected statues to these gods, prayed to them, and sacrificed animals and plants to them. They also honored the gods by building temples for them and obeying the pharaoh.

Moreover, the Egyptians believed in an afterlife. Every man and woman hoped that after death his or her soul would travel into the Underworld, ruled by the god Osiris. There, they believed, life would soon be comfortable and carefree. The Egyptians did not think the privilege of reaching the afterlife came without cost, however. Certain traditional, time-honored rituals had to be observed—or else the dead would not make it to Osiris's happy realm. That is why burial customs were extremely important to the Egyptians.

The Ever-Present Gods

It was equally important to Egyptians of all walks of life to show the proper respect for the gods and to worship them on a yearly, monthly, and sometimes daily basis. The reason for this was the belief that the gods were ever-present. According to Herodotus, Egypt "was ruled by gods who lived on earth amongst men, sometimes as one of them [i.e., the pharaoh, the living god]."[5]

Indeed, the Egyptians thought that one or more gods controlled or influenced nearly every phase of

A wall painting shows palace attendants carrying furniture to place in a pharaoh's tomb.

nature and daily life. Take Osiris, for example. He not only oversaw the afterlife, but also made the Nile flood each year and inspired the growth of crops and other plants. The goddess Isis, Osiris's sister, protected children; Hathor, pictured as a woman with a cow's head, was the goddess of love, dancing, and music; Thoth, who had a baboon's head, was the god of wisdom; and Anubis, with a jackal's head, guided people's souls to the afterlife.

Osiris's Spirit

The major difference between the pharaoh and all the other gods, of course, was that he could be seen, touched, and even killed; while the others were invisible and beyond death. The Egyptians explained this odd situation by citing a story central to their faith—that of Osiris's death and his spirit's rebirth. According to this tale, in the dim past the mighty sun-god Ra ordered Osiris to rule Egypt as its first king. But another god, Seth, Osiris's brother, was jealous. So he killed Osiris and stole the throne. Eventually, though, Osiris's son, Horus, overthrew Seth and became Egypt's rightful king. Thereafter, each year Osiris' spirit was reborn in the crops that grew in the spring. And Horus's spirit inhabited the living bodies of all the human pharaohs who followed him on the throne. Each pharaoh's death was seen as a reenactment of the death of Osiris. And the moment a pharaoh died, Horus' spirit entered the new pharaoh's body, while the old pharaoh's spirit became one with Osiris.

Osiris (left), ruler of the Underworld, and his son, the hawk-headed Horus, who avenged Osiris by killing Seth.

Prayer and Sacrifice

Worship of these gods took place during religious festivals held at set times of the year. But villages, families, and individuals often worshiped the gods more often. The two main forms of worship were prayer and sacrifice. Some prayers were general chants or hymns repeated from time to time to show respect and continued devotion. "Hail to you, Ra, Lord of Truth," one such prayer began. "You who hears the prayer of him who is in captivity . . . who saves the weak from the strong . . . you, great in love, at whose coming the people live." [6]

People also prayed for other reasons. A group or individual might pray for rain, for instance. Or a person might pray to find a husband or wife, or for an ill person to get well. A doctor attempting to heal someone might recite the prayer, "O Ra, God of light and health, inspire me,"[7] as he treated his patient.

Sacrifice, on the other hand, consisted of a material gift offered to a god or gods. While in Egypt, Herodotus observed some sacrifices and later described them in his famous history book. Set rituals had to be followed faithfully in all stages of the ceremony, he wrote. Before sacrificing a bull, for example, the priest carefully

> examines the animal, and if he finds a single black hair on him, pronounces him unclean [not fit for the sacrifice]. He goes over him

An illustration from the Egyptian Book of the Dead shows a woman worshiping a crocodile god.

with the greatest care. . . . If the animal passes all the tests successfully, the priest marks him . . . and the penalty is death for anybody who sacrifices an animal which has not been marked in this manner.[8]

Next, Herodotus listed the steps in the actual sacrifice of a bull:

They take the beast . . . to the appropriate altar and light a fire. Then, after pouring wine on the altar and calling the god by name, they slaughter the bull, cut off its head, and slice open the body. . . . When they have finished cutting up the bull, they first pray . . . and then stuff the body with loaves of bread, honey, raisins, figs . . . and other nice-smelling substances. Finally, they pour a quantity of oil over the body and burn it. . . . While the fire is consuming it, they beat their breasts.[9]

The Egyptians believed that the smoke from the burning bull rose up and fed the god. After thoroughly cooking the beast, the priests cut it into portions and served these to the worshipers.

Mummification and Burial

By performing such worship at certain times and leading a life that pleased the gods, the belief went, a person

A wall painting shows an Egyptian bull sacrifice.

had a good chance of reaching the afterlife after death. But once again, one had to follow the traditional rituals. First, the body had to be preserved. For those who could afford it, **mummification** was the best way to preserve a body. The **embalmers**, whose job was to turn a corpse into a mummy, first removed most of the internal organs. They placed these in a special jar. (Later, mourners placed the jar beside the mummy in the tomb.) The embalmers then put the body in a vat of **natrum**, a mineral salt, for seventy days. This removed most of the body's moisture. Next, Herodotus wrote, "the body is washed and then wrapped from head to foot in linen cut into strips and smeared on the underside with gum." [10]

Soon afterward, the family of the deceased laid the mummy in a wooden or stone coffin and placed the coffin in a tomb of brick or stone. Tombs were of various shapes and sizes, depending on the wealth of the family. The pharaohs and their relatives, of course, could afford the largest tombs of all. However, most Egyptians were poor farmers who could afford neither mummification nor tombs. The average family wrapped a body in a shroud of linen or reeds and buried it in a makeshift grave in the sand.

Whether rich or poor, all Egyptians buried food, clothes, tools, and/or other everyday items with the body. They believed that part of the dead person's soul would need these things to sustain itself in the grave or tomb.

In fact, in the long run it mattered little whether the burial was expensive or cheap, elaborate or simple. In the Egyptian religion, every person who lived a good life and followed the proper rituals could expect to reach Osiris's realm and achieve immortality. That deeply-held belief gave hope to the living and comfort to their families when they died.

Chapter Three

The Rise and Fall of the Egyptian Empire

During the years of the Old Kingdom, when most of the pyramids were built, Egypt remained more or less isolated from the rest of the world. This was mainly because the country was self-sufficient. It had vast supplies of crops and livestock raised by many hardworking farmers. Egypt also had a strong government run by the pharaoh and his advisers. Under their guidance, society was orderly and productive. Both leaders and their subjects seemed content with their lives and largely ignored the outside world.

Eventually, though, the Egyptians became major players on the world's political stage. They expanded their horizons outward, both to the south and northeast, and conquered their immediate neighbors. The Egyptian empire grew, and now Egyptian soldiers manned forts in faraway lands. But like all great empires in history, the Egyptian empire was destined to fall apart. And once the Egyptians lost their empire, they were never able to regain it.

Farmers harvest their crops in these wall paintings. Egypt produced vast amounts of food, making it self-sufficient.

Expansion Through War and Trade

The story of Egypt's rise and fall as a great power begins not long after the start of the period and realm now called the Middle Kingdom. It lasted from about 2050 to 1650 B.C., about four centuries. The pharaohs of the Twelfth Dynasty marched their armies into Nubia, the land lying directly south of Egypt, and soon made it (Nubia) a province in a growing Egyptian empire.

Egypt not only made the Nubians work for them, but they also grew wealthier from the gold they extracted from Nubian mines. Mining was extremely difficult, dangerous, and thankless work. And it usually broke both the bodies and spirits of the miners, who were mostly slaves, war captives, or convicted criminals. A later Greek geographer named Agatharchides penned this bleak description of life in an Egyptian gold mine:

> Those who are young and strong quarry the gleaming stone with metal picks. . . . They cut numerous tunnels in the rock. . . . Young boys creeping through the tunnels . . . collect what has fallen on the floor and carry it outside [where men and woman use hammers to break up the rocks containing the gold]. They are a sad sight, their cloths pulled up just enough to cover their private parts. . . . All who suffer this fate, feel that death is more desirable than life.[11]

Though richer than ever from this gold, the pharaohs of the Twelfth Dynasty sought even more wealth, as well as various luxury goods. So they expanded trade relations to the north and northeast. By land and sea, Egyptian traders exploited foreign markets, including those in Palestine (the area now occupied by Israel and Lebanon); Syria (north of Palestine); and the large Greek island of Crete. Through conquest and trade, Egypt gained a reputation as a nation to be reckoned with.

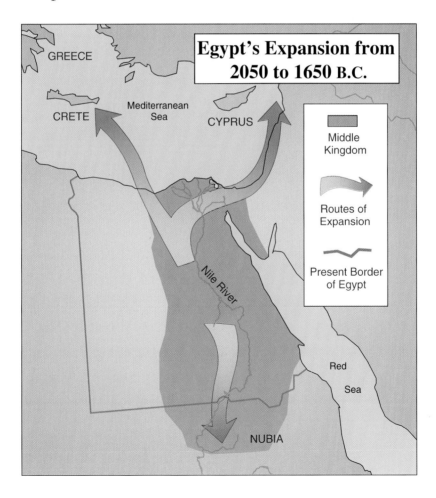

A Need for Better Weapons

Then, beginning in the eighteenth century B.C., a series of unexpected setbacks damaged Egypt's power and prosperity. **Civil conflicts** broke out between various Egyptian cities and regions. Also, Nubia broke free of Egyptian control. Worst of all, an army of foreigners, an Asian people called the Hyksos, invaded from the northeast and took over large parts of northern Egypt.

A key factor in the Hyksos's success was that their army was superior to the Egyptian army. Before this time, Egyptian soldiers wore no armor. They carried shields made of wood covered with cowhide, and their main weapons were clubs, axes, and bows and arrows. By contrast, Hyksos soldiers had body armor, metal swords, and stronger shields. They also possessed horse-drawn chariots. These vehicles smashed through the Egyptian battle lines, killing many and sending others fleeing.

The Egyptians studied and copied this new kind of warfare. And before long, they had thousands of metal swords and battle chariots of their own. An ancient document describing an Egyptian charioteer of this era has survived and tells about taking a chariot to a special workshop for repairs:

They take care of your chariot so that [the wheels are] no longer loose. . . . They fix up your **yoke** [the part that attaches the chariot to the horses' harnesses]. They apply your ensign

This wall painting shows an Egyptian pharaoh leading his troops to victory.

[personal emblem or symbol], engraved with a chisel, and they put a handle on your whip and attach a lash to it. [Then] you sally forth quickly to fight . . . and accomplish glorious deeds.[12]

The Glorious New Kingdom

Using Egypt's new and improved army, Ahmose I, the first pharaoh of the Eighteenth Dynasty, drove the Hyksos out of the country. His successors, Amenhotep I and Thutmose I, recaptured Nubia and attacked parts of Palestine and Syria. The conquering pharaohs proudly recorded their exploits in numerous **inscriptions**. One surviving example reads: "He [the pharaoh] bound the heads of [his enemies]. . . . He has

27

A statue captures the likeness of the great warrior pharaoh Thutmose III.

gathered them all into his fist, [and] his **mace** [club] has crashed upon their heads." [13]

The advent of the Eighteenth Dynasty marked the beginning of what modern scholars call the New Kingdom. It lasted from about 1550 to 1070 B.C., almost five centuries. In this period, Egypt built a true empire. The greatest warrior-pharaoh of them all was Thutmose III (who reigned 1479–1425 B.C.). He is sometimes called the "Egyptian Alexander the Great," after the famous ancient Greek conqueror. Thutmose subdued Palestine and Syria. He even dared to attack (though he did not capture) the powerful kingdom of Mitanni, situated northeast of Syria. Under Thutmose's rule, the Egyptian Empire at its largest covered an area of about four hundred thousand square miles—almost twice the size of the state of Texas.

The Memory of Egypt's Greatness

Eventually, however, Egypt's power declined. New **civil disputes** among the Egyptians themselves was one cause. A series of pharaohs—who were weak, inept, or both—was another. In addition, some of

Egypt's enemies began using iron swords and other weapons. These were much stronger and more deadly than the copper and **bronze** ones the Egyptians had. Since the Egyptians had no natural sources of iron, they were at a severe disadvantage.

The New Kingdom ended, therefore, as foreign powers attacked and seized control of Egypt. Among them were the Assyrians and Persians (from what are now Iraq and Iran). Later, the Greeks, led by Alexander the Great himself, also entered Egypt. Not long after Alexander's death (in 323 B.C.), one of his generals, Ptolemy, crowned himself pharaoh and established a new dynasty—the Ptolemaic.

This Greek dynasty turned out to be Egypt's last. Most of the Ptolemies were weak rulers. And by the first century B.C., the country was a third-rate power hiding in the orbit of the most powerful nation the world had yet seen—Rome. From their homeland in Italy, the Romans ruled or threatened all the lands surrounding the Mediterranean Sea.

The last Ptolemaic ruler, the famous Cleopatra VII, tried to revive Egypt's greatness. She and Mark Antony, a Roman general and ally, challenged another powerful Roman, Octavian, but were defeated in a huge sea battle at Actium, in Greece, in 31 B.C. Octavian then seized Egypt, taking a new name—Augustus, "the **revered** one"—and established the mighty Roman Empire. And Egypt, its former greatness now only a memory, became one of Rome's many provinces.

Chapter Four

The Modern Rediscovery of Ancient Egypt

Rome's grand empire, like Egypt's, eventually fell. And its former provinces, including Egypt, were left to fend for themselves. As the centuries rolled by, Egypt remained a poor, largely backward land. No one bothered to repair its once magnificent palaces and statues. So they steadily decayed. Meanwhile, thieves looted most of the treasures from the pyramids and other tombs. In time, the Egyptians forgot about, or no longer cared about, their glorious ancient **heritage**.

Then, in the 1700s and 1800s, the modern world began to rediscover Egypt's lost heritage. Various scholars, including members of the new science of **archaeology** (the study of past civilizations), traveled to Egypt. They examined the pyramids and other remaining structures in detail. And they dug into the country's sands and unearthed numerous artifacts that had not been seen in thousands of years. It soon became clear that a splendid, impressive civilization had once existed in Egypt. Today, hundreds of thousands of people come from around the world to marvel at the relics of this country's past.

French Discoveries Awaken the Past

The modern rediscovery of Egypt began when the French conqueror Napoléon invaded the country in 1798. In addition to his soldiers, Napoléon brought along 167 scholars. He ordered them to examine the land's plants and animals and also its

Modern tourists at the pyramids at Giza, which are among the most popular attractions in the world.

surviving ancient monuments. The French scholars and soldiers were plainly stunned by the size and grandeur of some of these structures. One of the French scholars, Baron Vivant Denon, recorded their reactions. When Napoléon's troops sailed down the Nile and first saw the remains of an ancient Egyptian palace, Denon wrote, "the whole army, suddenly and with one accord [all together], stood in amazement . . . and clapped their hands with delight."[14] In 1802, Denon published his book, *A Journey Through Upper and Lower Egypt.* This popular volume brought Egypt's relics to the attention of Europe's scholarly community and reading public.

At the same time, one particular Egyptian artifact made headlines around the world. In 1799, Napoléon's men found a stone covered with ancient inscriptions. Because it rested in the small town of Rosetta, in northern Egypt, it became known as the

Rosetta Stone. The stone bore inscriptions of the same message in more than one language. One of these was ancient Greek and another was hieroglyphics, the picture language used by the ancient Egyptians.

The famous Rosetta Stone was the key that unlocked the secret of hieroglyphics.

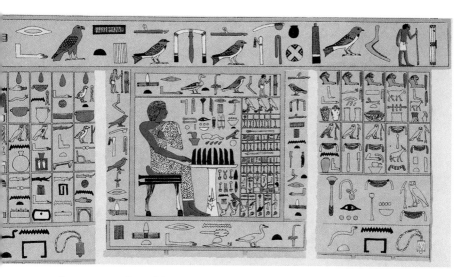

An example of hieroglyphics from a tomb appears above.

Before this, modern scholars had no clue about how to read hieroglyphics. But they *could* read ancient Greek. A French scholar named Jean-François Champollion compared the Greek letters of the message to the hieroglyphs of that same text. And through painstaking work, he managed to decipher the ancient Egyptian language. For the first time in over a thousand years, people could read the inscriptions found on monuments all over Egypt. In 1828–1829, Champollion and other scholars traveled throughout the country, recording and translating all the hieroglyphics they could find.

The Golden Age of Egyptology

Scholarly interest in ancient Egypt became so great that a separate branch of archaeology formed— **Egyptology**. Throughout the nineteenth century,

French, English, German, and other scholars continued to uncover and study Egyptian artifacts. In the late 1800s, for example, an Englishman, Sir William Flinders Petrie, traveled to Egypt. He supervised the first detailed scientific investigation of the Great Pyramid of Khufu. And from his studies, scholars began to understand the methods used by its builders.

But as important as they were, all these efforts paled in comparison to the work done by scholars in the twentieth century. In fact, the first half of that century is often called the "golden age" of Egyptology. French scholar Pierre Montet made one of the more important discoveries. In 1928, he began excavating at Tanis, in the Nile delta. And in 1939, he uncovered a series of underground chambers containing the remains of three pharaohs of the Twenty-first and Twenty-second Dynasties (ca.1070–715 B.C.). Every other royal tomb unearthed in Egypt had been raided by robbers. What made this find so special was that the tombs were undisturbed. The rulers' mummies, along with some golden jewelry, bowls, and cups, all rested exactly where they had been placed three thousand years before.

"Wonderful Things"

Without question, the most important and famous discovery made in Egypt of that or any era was the tomb of the pharaoh Tutankhamen. The world came to call him "King Tut" for short. A ruler who

Dr. Pierre Montet examines one of the three mummies he discovered at Tanis in 1939.

died young and accomplished little, he reigned from 1336 to 1327 B.C., during the Eighteenth Dynasty. In 1922, English archaeologist Howard Carter was digging in the Valley of the Kings, a rocky area located a few hundred miles south of Giza. Several pharaohs had ordered their remains buried there in secret to keep them safe from robbers, but the thieves found and looted the tombs anyway.

As Carter's excavations revealed, though, Tut's tomb had not suffered much. In fact, almost all of its contents were still completely intact. Moreover, the splendor and sheer number of these artifacts far surpassed any found in Egypt before or since. Carter

The golden funerary mask of King Tut, unearthed by scholar Howard Carter in the 1920s.

later recalled the exciting moment when he first gazed into the tomb's front chamber:

> At first I could see nothing, the hot air escaping from the chamber causing the candle to flicker, but presently, as my eyes grew accus-

tomed to the light, details of the room emerged slowly from the mist, strange animals, statues, and gold—everywhere the glint of gold. . . . I was struck dumb with amazement, and when Lord Carnarvon [Carter's colleague] . . . inquired anxiously, "Can you see anything?", it was all I could do to get out the words, "Yes, wonderful things!" [15]

In time, Carter and his team found that these "wonderful things" included more than two thousand priceless relics. Among them was Tut's mummy, lying within a coffin of solid gold weighing 2,448 pounds! Also brought to light were life-size statues of Tut, furniture, swords and other weapons, exquisite gold jewelry, musical instruments, full-sized boats, and more. Today, these and other magnificent relics from Egypt's past can be seen in museums in Cairo, London, Paris, and other cities. They attest to the talents, achievements, triumphs, and tragedies of a truly great people who vanished long ago.

Notes

Chapter One: The Lives of Egypt's God-Kings

1. Quoted in Lionel Casson, *Ancient Egypt*. New York: Time-Life, 1965, p. 36.
2. Quoted in Lionel Casson, *Daily Life in Ancient Egypt*. New York: American Heritage, 1975, p. 49.
3. Quoted in Casson, *Daily Life*, p. 50.
4. Herodotus, *The Histories*, trans. Aubrey de Sélincourt. New York: Penguin Books, 1972, p. 179.

Chapter Two: Egyptian Worship and Burial

5. Herodotus, *Histories*, p. 187.
6. Quoted in Richard Patrick, *All Color Book of Egyptian Mythology*. London: Octopus Books, 1972, p. 13.
7. Quoted in Lewis Spence, *Ancient Egyptian Myths and Legends*. New York: Dover Publications, 1990, p. 269.
8. Herodotus, *Histories*, p. 144.
9. Herodotus, *Histories*, pp. 144–45.
10. Herodotus, *Histories*, p. 161.

Chapter Three: The Rise and Fall of the Egyptian Empire

11. Quoted in Casson, *Daily Life*, p. 77.
12. Quoted in Ian Shaw, *Egyptian Warfare and Weapons*. Buckinghamshire, UK: Shire Publications, 1991, pp. 41–42.

13. Quoted in Shaw, *Egyptian Warfare and Weapons*, p. 9.

Chapter Four: The Modern Rediscovery of Ancient Egypt

14. Quoted in Paul G. Bahn, ed., *The Cambridge Illustrated History of Archaeology*. New York: Cambridge University Press, 1996, p. 69.

15. Quoted in Desmond Stewart, *The Pyramids and the Sphinx*. New York: Newsweek Book Division, 1971, p. 121.

Glossary

archaeology: the study of past civilizations and their artifacts

bronze: an alloy (mixture) of the metals copper and tin

civil conflicts or disputes: arguments and/or fighting among the leaders and people of one country

dynasty: a series of rulers belonging to one family line

Egyptology: the branch of archaeology dealing specifically with ancient Egypt

embalmers: people who prepare dead bodies for burial

heritage: ideas and works passed on from a culture to the cultures that follow it

inscriptions: letters and words carved into stone

mace: a club used in warfare

mummification: a process in which a human or animal body is prepared and preserved before burial

natrum (or natron): a mineral salt used by ancient embalmers to dry out bodies and thereby better preserve them

pharaoh: the supposedly semi-divine ruler of ancient Egypt

revered: held in great respect or awe, or worshiped

sacrifice: a material gift offered to a god or gods; or the act of making such a gift

yoke: a device for attaching a horse's harness to a chariot or wagon

For Further Exploration

George Hart, *Ancient Egypt*. New York: Time-Life, 1995. A very colorfully illustrated introduction to the wonders of ancient Egypt for young readers.

Tim McNeese, *The Pyramids of Giza*. San Diego: Lucent Books, 1997. This well-written volume explains in considerable detail why and how the Egyptian pyramids were built, as well as who built them.

Anne Millard, *Mysteries of the Pyramids*. Brookfield, CT: Copper Beach Books, 1995. Aimed at basic readers, this book by a noted scholar is short but brightly illustrated and filled with interesting facts about the pyramids and ancient Egyptian life.

Neil Morris, *Atlas of Ancient Egypt*. New York: NTC Contemporary Publishing, 2000. This excellent book about ancient Egypt contains many maps and also several impressive double-page spreads of specific eras and aspects of everyday life. Highly recommended.

David Murdock, *Tutankhamun: The Life and Death of a Pharaoh*. London: Dorling Kindersley, 1998. A beautifully illustrated examination of an Egyptian ruler who died young and was later forgotten, only to become famous in modern times when scholars unearthed his tomb.

Don Nardo, ed., *Cleopatra*. San Diego: Greenhaven Press, 2001. The reading level of this volume is challenging for grade school students but well worth the effort. In a series of short essays, noted scholars tell nearly all that is known about this famous queen and her exploits.

———, *Egyptian Mythology*. Berkeley Heights, NJ: Enslow Publishers, 2001. Aimed at intermediate readers, this book retells some of the most famous Egyptian myths, including the story of Osiris's murder by Seth.

———, *The Importance of Cleopatra*. San Diego: Lucent Books, 1994. A general survey of Cleopatra's background, love affairs, strengths as a ruler, death, and the many modern literary and artistic works inspired by her story.

Kelly Trumble, *Cat Mummies*. Boston: Houghton Mifflin, 1999. An unusual and nicely illustrated volume that tells why cats were important in ancient Egyptian society and how these animals were mummified.

Index

Actium, 29
afterlife
  Anubis and, 16
  beliefs about, 21
  mummification and,
    20–21
  Osiris and, 14
  Underworld and, 14
Agatharchides, 24
Ahmose I (pharaoh),
  27, 28
Alexander the Great, 29
Amenhotep I
  (pharaoh), 27–28
Anubis (god), 16
archaeology, 30–31
Assyrians, 29
Augustus, 29

Balcony of Appearances,
  11
burial, 19–21

Carnarvon, Lord, 37
Carter, Howard, 35–37
Champollion, Jean-
  François, 33

civil disputes, 26, 28
Cleopatra VII (queen),
  29
Crete, 25

Denon, Vivant, 32
dynasties, 8
  Eighteenth, 27–28, 35
  Ptolemaic, 29
  Twelfth, 24–25
  Twenty-first, 34
  Twenty-second, 34

Egypt
  unification of, 8
"Egyptian Alexander
  the Great," 28
Egyptian Empire
  fall of, 28–29
  growth of, 27–28
  rise of, 24–25
  under Thutmose III,
    28
Egyptology, 33–34
embalmers, 20

Giza, 4, 11

gods and goddesses
  importance of, 14,
    15–16
  pharaohs as, 8, 16
gold mining, 24
Great Pyramid, 11, 34
Greeks, 29

Hathor (goddess), 16
Herodotus
  about gods, 15
  about the Great
    Pyramid, 11
  about mummification,
    20
  about sacrifices, 18–19
hieroglyphics, 32–33
homes, 9, 11
Horus (god), 16
Hyksos, 26, 27

Isis (goddess), 16

*Journey Through Upper
  and Lower Egypt, A*
  (Denon), 32

Khufu (pharaoh), 11,
  34
King Tut

reign of, 34–35
tomb of, 35–37

Mark Antony, 29
Memphis, 8
Menes (pharaoh), 8–9
Middle Kingdom, 24
mining, 24
Mitanni, 28
Montet, Pierre, 34
mummification, 20–21,
  37

Napoléon, 31–32
natrum, 20
New Kingdom, 27–29
Nile River
  importance of, 5–6
  Osiris and, 16
  path of, 4–5
Nubia, 24, 26

Octavian, 29
Old Kingdom, 11, 22
Osiris (god)
  Nile River and, 16
  pharaoh and, 16
  Underworld and, 14

Palestine, 25, 28

people
  homes of, 9
  as workers, 13
Persians, 29
Petrie, Sir William
  Flinders, 34
pharaohs, 4
  crowning of, 10
  as gods, 8, 16
  lives of, 8–10
  Osiris and, 16
  see also individual
    names of pharaohs
picture language, 32–33
prayer, 17–18
princes, 9–11
Ptolemy (pharaoh), 29
pyramids, 4
  archaeology and,
    34–37
  building of, 11–12
  looting of, 30, 35
  workers on, 13

Ra (god), 8, 16
religion
  afterlife, 14, 16, 20–21
  gods and goddesses, 8,
    14, 15–16

importance of, 14
prayer and, 17–18
sacrifice and, 17,
  18–19
Rome, 29
Rosetta Stone, 32–33

sacrifice, 17, 18–19
Seth (god), 16
Syria, 25, 28

Tanis, 34
Thoth (god), 16
Thutmose I (pharaoh),
  27–28
Thutmose III
  (pharaoh), 10–11, 28
trade, 25
Tutankhamen (pharaoh)
  reign of, 34–35
  tomb of, 35–37

Underworld, 14

Valley of the Kings, 35

wars, 24, 26–28, 29
weapons, 26–27, 29
writing, 32–33

Picture Credits

About the Author

A historian and award-winning writer, Don Nardo has written and edited numerous books about the ancient world. Among these are *Life in Ancient Athens, Greek and Roman Sport, Egyptian Mythology,* and Greenhaven Press's massive *Complete History of Ancient Greece* and *A-Z Encyclopedia of Ancient Rome.* He lives with his wife, Christine, in Massachusetts.